Break the Power of Negative Words

JOHN BEVERE

Books about Spirit-Led Living

The Inner Strength Series
LIVING WITH STRENGTH IN TODAY'S WORLD

BREAK THE POWER OF NEGATIVE WORDS by John Bevere
Published by Charisma House
A part of Strang Communications Company
600 Rinehart Road
Lake Mary, Florida 32746
www.charismahouse.com

Unless otherwise noted, all Scripture quotations are from the
New King James Version of the Bible. Copyright © 1979,
1980, 1982 by Thomas Nelson, Inc., publishers. Used by permission.

Scripture quotations marked KJV are from the King James
Version of the Bible.

Cover design by Rachel Campbell

Library of Congress Catalog Card Number: 2001098128
International Standard Book Number: 0-88419-835-9

02 03 04 05   87654321
Printed in the United States of America

Contents

Introduction

The disciples of Jesus witnessed many great and notable miracles. They watched in amazement as blind eyes were opened and the dead were raised. They heard Jesus command a life-threatening storm to stillness. They saw thousands fed by the miracle of multiplication of a few loaves and fishes. The list of Jesus' miracles and wonders were so inexhaustible that, according to the Bible, the world of books could not contain it.

Never before had mankind witnessed the miraculous hand of God in such an overwhelming and tangible way. Amazed and awed as the disciples were, it was not these miracles that pushed them to the brink of doubt. No, that challenge would come later toward the end of Jesus' earthly ministry. Jesus had instructed His disciples, "If your brother sins against you…seven times in a day, and seven times in a day returns to you, saying, 'I repent,' you shall forgive him." Their immediate response to the Lord was, "Increase our faith" (Luke 17:3–5). The miracles had not inspired a cry for greater faith—but the simple command to forgive those who have wronged you did!

Jesus said, "It is impossible that no offenses should come…" (Luke 17:1). It is not a question of opportunity to be offended, but what your response will be. It is an unfortunate fact that not some, but many are offended and held captive.

> # The most effective way for the enemy to blind us is to cause us to focus on ourselves.

Satan is not as blatant as many believe. He is subtle and delights in deception. He is shrewd in his operations, cunning and crafty. He can disguise himself as a messenger of light. If we are not trained by the Word of God to divide rightly between good and evil, we won't recognize his traps for what they are.

One of his most deceptive and insidious kinds of bait is something every Christian has encountered—offense. Actually, offense itself is not deadly—if it stays in the trap. But if we pick it up, consume it and feed on it in our hearts, then we have become offended. Offended people produce much fruit, such as hurt, anger, outrage, jealousy, resentment, strife, bitterness, hatred and envy. Some of the consequences of picking up an offense are insults, attacks, wounding, division, separation, broken relationships, betrayal and backsliding.

Often those who are offended do not even realize they are trapped. They are oblivious to their condition because they are so focused on the wrong that was done to them. They are in denial. The most effective way for the enemy to blind us is to cause us to focus on ourselves.

Freedom from the power of negative words of offense is essential for every Christian, because Jesus said it is impossible to live this life and not have the opportunity to be offended (Luke 17:1).

Adapted from John Bevere, *The Bait of Satan* (Lake Mary, FL: Charisma House, 1997), ix–xiv.

ONE

Don't Become a
Spiritual Vagabond

DEVELOPING
Inner Strength

I was in one church for several years. The pastor was one of the best preachers in America. When I first attended that church, I would sit with my mouth open in awe of the biblical teaching that came from his mouth.

As time passed, because of my position of serving the pastor, I was close enough to see his flaws. I questioned some of his ministry decisions. I became critical and judgmental, and offense set in. He preached, and I sensed no inspiration or anointing. His preaching no longer ministered to me.

Another couple with whom we were friends and also served together on staff seemed to be discerning the same thing. God sent them out from the church, and they started their own ministry. They asked us to go with them. They knew how we were struggling. They encouraged us to get on with the call on our lives. They would tell us all the things this pastor, his wife and the leadership were doing wrong. We would commiserate together, feeling hopeless and trapped.

They seemed sincerely concerned for our welfare. But our discussions only fueled our fire of discontent and offense. As Proverbs 26:20 illustrates, "Where there is no wood, the fire goes out; and where there is no talebearer, strife ceases." What they were saying to us may have been correct information, but it was wrong in the eyes of God because it was adding wood to the fire of offense in them as well as in us.

"We know you are a man of God," they said to me. "That's why you are having the problems you are having in this place." It sounded good.

My wife and I said to each other, "That is it. We are in a bad situation. We need to get out. This pastor and his wife love us. They will pastor us. The people in their church will receive us and the ministry God has given us."

We left our church and began attending this couple's church, but only for a few short months. Even though we thought we had run from our problem, we noticed we were still struggling. Our spirits had no joy. We were bound to a fear of becoming what we had just left. It seemed everything we did was forced and unnatural. We couldn't fit into the flow of the Spirit. Now even our relationship with the new pastor and his wife was strained.

Finally I knew we should return to our home church. When we did, we knew at once that we were back in the will of God, even though it had appeared that we would be more accepted and loved elsewhere.

Then God shocked me. "John, I never told you to leave this church. You left out of offense!"

This was not the fault of the other pastor and his wife, but ours. They understood our frustration and were trying to resolve the same issues in their own hearts. When you're out of the will of God, you will not be a blessing or help to any church. When you're out of the will of God, even the good relationships will be strained. We had been out of God's will.

D avid was mistreated by Saul, the man he had hoped would be a father to him. David kept trying to understand where he had gone wrong. What had he done to turn Saul's heart against him, and how could he win it back? He proved his loyalty by sparing Saul's life even though Saul aggressively pursued his.

He cried out to Saul with his head bowed to the ground, saying, "See that there is neither evil nor rebellion in my hand, and I have not sinned against you" (1 Sam. 24:11).

Once David knew he had shown his loyalty to his leader, his mind was eased. Later he learned more devastating news—Saul still desired to destroy him. But David refused to raise a hand against the one who sought to take his life, although God had put the army to sleep and had given David a companion who pleaded for permission to kill Saul. David somehow sensed that this sleeping army served another purpose—the testing of his very heart.

God wanted to see whether David would kill to establish his kingdom after the order of Saul or whether he would allow God to establish his throne in righteousness forever.

Beloved, do not avenge yourselves, but

rather give place to wrath; for it is written, "Vengeance is Mine, I will repay," says the Lord.

—Romans 12:19

It is righteous for God to avenge His servants. It is unrighteous for God's servants to avenge themselves. Saul was a man who avenged himself. He chased David, a man of honor, for fourteen years and murdered the priests and their families.

God tests His servants with obedience.

As David stood over the sleeping Saul, he faced an important test. It would reveal whether David still had the noble heart of a shepherd or the insecurity of another Saul. Would he remain a man after God's heart? Initially it seems so much easier to take matters into our own hands rather than to wait on a righteous God.

God tests His servants with obedience. He deliberately places us in situations where the standards of religion and society would appear to justify our actions. He allows others, especially those close to us, to encourage us to protect ourselves. We may even think we would be noble and protect others by avenging ourselves. But this is not God's way. It is the way of the world's wisdom. It is earthly and fleshly.

How Can God Use Corrupt Leaders?

Many people ask, "Why does God put people under leaders who make serious mistakes and even some that are wicked?"

Look at the childhood of Samuel. (See 1 Samuel 2–5.) God, not the devil, was the One who put this young man under the authority of a corrupt priest named Eli and his two wicked sons, Hophni and Phinehas, who were priests as well. These men were very wicked. They took offerings by manipulation and force, and they committed fornication with the women who assembled at the door of the tabernacle.

Can you imagine if you were serving a minister who lived this kind of life? A minister who was so insensitive to the things of the Spirit that he couldn't recognize a woman in prayer and accused her of being drunk! So fleshly that he was grossly overweight. So compromising he did nothing about his sons, whom he had appointed as leaders, who were committing fornication right in the church.

Most Christians today would be offended and search for another church, telling others as they went of the wicked lifestyle of their former pastor and his leaders. In the midst of such corruption, I love the report of what young Samuel did: "Now the boy Samuel ministered to the LORD before Eli" (1 Sam. 3:1).

But corruption took its toll: "And the word of the LORD was rare in those days; there was no widespread revelation" (v. 1). God seemed distant to the entire Hebrew community. The lamp of God was about to go out in the temple of the Lord. Yet did Samuel go look for another place to worship? Did he go to the elders to expose the wickedness of Eli and his sons? Did he form a committee to put Eli and his sons out of the pastorate? No, he ministered to the Lord!

God had placed Samuel there, and he was not responsible for the behavior of Eli or his sons. He was put under them not to judge them but to serve them. He knew Eli was God's servant, not his. He knew that God was quite capable of dealing with His own.

Samuel served God's appointed minister the best he could, without the pressure to judge him or correct him. The only time Samuel spoke a word of correction was when Eli came to Samuel and asked him what prophecy God had given him the night before. Even then it was not a word of correction from Samuel, but from God. If more people would get hold of this truth, our churches would be different.

The Planted Flourish

The Bible says in Psalm 92:13, "Those who are *planted* in the house of the LORD *shall flourish* in the courts of our God" (emphasis added).

Notice that those who flourish are "planted" in the house of the Lord. What happens to a plant if you transplant it every three weeks? Most of you know that its root system will diminish, and it will not blossom or prosper. If you keep transplanting it, the plant will die of shock!

Many people go from church to church, ministry team to ministry team, trying to develop their ministry. If God puts them in a place where they are not recognized and encouraged, they are easily offended. If they don't agree with the way something is done, they are offended and leave, blaming the leadership. They are blind to any of their own character flaws and do not realize God wanted to refine and mature them through the pressure they were under.

Let's learn from the examples God gives with plants and trees. When a fruit tree is put in the ground it has to face rainstorms, hot sun and wind. If a young tree could talk, it might say, "Please get me out of here! Put me in a place where there is no sweltering heat or windy storms!"

If the gardener listened to the tree, he would actually harm it. Trees endure the hot sun and rainstorms by sending their roots down deeper. The adversity they face is eventually the source of great stability. The harshness of the elements surrounding them causes them to seek another source of life. They will one day come to the place that even the greatest of windstorms cannot affect their ability to produce fruit.

A few years ago I lived in Florida, a citrus capital.

Most Floridians know that the colder the winter is for the trees, the sweeter the oranges. If we did not run so fast from spiritual resistance, our root systems would have a chance to become stronger and deeper, and our fruit would be plentiful and sweeter in the eyes of God and more palatable to His people! We would be mature trees that the Lord delights in rather than ones uprooted for their lack of fruit (Luke 13:6–9). We should not resist the very thing God sends to mature us.

The psalmist David, inspired by the Holy Spirit, made a powerful connection between offense, the law of God and our spiritual growth. He wrote in Psalm 1:1–2:

> Blessed is the man…[whose] delight is in the law of the Lord; and in His law he meditates day and night.

Then in Psalm 119:165, he gave us more insight into people who love God's laws.

> Great peace have they which love [or delight in] thy law: and nothing shall *offend* them.
>
> —KJV, EMPHASIS ADDED

Verse 3 of Psalm 1 finally describes the destiny of such a person.

> He shall be like a *tree* planted by the rivers of water, that brings forth its fruit in its season, whose leaf also shall not wither; and whatever he does shall prosper.
>
> —EMPHASIS ADDED

In other words, a believer who chooses to delight in the Word of God in the midst of adversity will avoid being offended. That person will be like a tree whose roots search deep to where the Spirit provides strength and nourishment. He will draw from the well of God deep within his spirit. This will mature him to the point where adversity will now be the catalyst for fruit. Hallelujah!

Now we gain insight into Jesus' interpretation of the parable of the sower.

> And these are they likewise which are sown on stony ground; who, when they have heard the word, immediately receive it with gladness; and have no root in themselves, and so *endure* but for a time: afterward, when affliction or persecution ariseth for

the word's sake, *immediately they are offended.*

—MARK 4:16–17, KJV, EMPHASIS ADDED

Once you leave the place God has chosen for you, your root system begins to dwarf. The next time it will be easier for you to flee from adversity because you have been careful *not* to root yourself deeply. You end up coming to the place where you have little or no strength to endure hardship or persecution.

A believer who chooses to delight in the Word of God in the midst of adversity will avoid being offended.

You then become a spiritual vagabond, wandering from place to place, suspicious and afraid that others will mistreat you. Crippled and hindered in your ability to produce true spiritual fruit, you struggle in a self-centered life, eating the remains of the fruit of others.

Look at Cain and Abel, the first sons of Adam.

Cain brought an offering to the Lord from the works of his own hands, the fruit of his vineyard. It was brought forth with much toil. He had to clear the ground of rocks, stumps and other debris. He had to plow and cultivate the soil. He had to plant, water, fertilize and protect his crops. He put much effort in his service toward God. But it was his own sacrifice rather than obedience toward God's way. It symbolized the worship of God by one's own strength and ability rather than by God's grace.

Abel, on the other hand, brought an offering of obedience, the choice firstborn of his flock and their fat. He did not labor as Cain did to bring this forth, but it was dear to him. Both brothers would have heard how their mother and father had attempted to cover their nakedness with fig leaves, which represented their own works to cover their sin. But God demonstrated acceptable sacrifice by covering Adam and Eve with the skin of an innocent animal. Adam and Eve were ignorant of this unacceptable covering of their sin. But having been shown God's way, they were no longer ignorant, nor were their children.

Cain had tried to win God's acceptance apart

from His counsel. God responded by showing He would accept those who came to Him under His parameters of grace (Abel's sacrifice) and would reject what was attempted under the domain of the "knowledge of good and evil" (Cain's religious works). He then instructed Cain that if he would do good, he'd be accepted, but if he would not choose life, then sin would master him.

Cain was offended with the Lord. Rather than repent and do what was right, allowing this situation to strengthen his character, he vented on Abel his anger and offense with God. He murdered Abel. God said to Cain:

> So now you are cursed from the earth, which has opened its mouth to receive your brother's blood from your hand. When you till the ground, it shall *no longer yield its strength to you*. A *fugitive* and a *vagabond* you shall be on the earth.
> —GENESIS 4:11–12, EMPHASIS ADDED

The thing Cain feared most, to be rejected by God, he brought as a judgment on himself. The very medium through which he tried to win God's approval was now cursed by his own hand. The bloodshed now brought a curse. The ground would no longer give up its strength to him. Fruit would come only through great effort.

Offended Christians cut off their own ability to produce fruit. In the parable of the sower, Jesus compared the heart with soil. Just as Cain's fields were barren, the soil of an offended heart is barren, poisoned by bitterness. Offended people still may experience miracles, words of utterance, strong preaching and healing in their lives. But these are gifts of the Spirit, not fruit. We will be judged according to fruit, not gifting. A gift is given. Fruit is cultivated.

Offended Christians cut off their own ability to produce fruit.

Notice that God said Cain would become a fugitive and a vagabond as a result of his actions. There are numerous spiritual fugitives and vagabonds in our churches today. Their gifts of singing, preaching, prophesying and so on are not received by the leadership in their previous church, so off they go. They are running aimlessly and carry an offense, looking for that perfect church that will receive their gift and heal their hurts.

They feel beat up and persecuted. They feel as if they are modern-day Jeremiahs. It is "just them and God," with everyone else out to get them. They become unteachable. They get what I call a *persecution complex*—"Everyone is out to get me." They comfort themselves that they are just persecuted saints or prophets of God. They are suspicious of everyone. This is exactly what happened to Cain. Look what he says:

> I shall be a fugitive and a vagabond on the earth, and *it will happen that anyone who finds me will kill me.*
> —Genesis 4:14, emphasis added

Consider that Cain had the persecution complex—everyone was out to get him! It is the same today. Offended people believe everyone is out to get them. With this attitude it is difficult for them to see areas in their own lives that need change. They isolate themselves and conduct themselves in such a manner that invites abuse.

> A man who isolates himself seeks his own
> desire; he rages against all wise judgment.
> —Proverbs 18:1

God never created us to live separately and independently of each other. He likes it when His children care for and nurture each other. He is frustrated when we sulk and feel sorry for ourselves, making everyone else responsible for our happiness. He wants us to be active members of the family. He wants us to get our life from Him. An isolated person seeks only his own desire, not God's. He receives no counsel and sets himself up for deception.

God never created us to live separately and independently of each other.

I am not talking about seasons in which God calls individuals apart to equip and refresh them. I'm describing those who have imprisoned themselves. They wander from church to church, relationship to relationship, and isolate themselves in their own world. They think that all who do not agree with them are wrong and are against them. They protect themselves in their isolation and feel safe in the controlled environment they have set up for themselves. They no longer have to confront their own character flaws. Rather than facing the difficulties, they try to escape the test. The character development that comes as the result of working through conflicts with others is lost as the cycle of offense begins again.

Adapted from *The Bait of Satan*, 47–58.

TWO

Face Reality

DEVELOPING
Inner Strength

A man who had previously worked for another minister came to work for our ministry team. He had been hurt by his former leader, but time had passed. I felt the Lord was leading me to ask him to come work with us. I believed he was in the process of overcoming this hurt.

I called his former employer and shared my plans to bring him on staff. He encouraged me and thought it was a good move because he knew I cared for both of them. He believed the healing could be completed while he worked with us. I told both men that my prayer was for restoration and healing in their relationship.

When the man joined our ministry team, there were problems almost immediately. I'd address the issue only to see temporary relief. It seemed he couldn't get beyond his former relationship. It kept coming back to haunt him. He even accused me of doing the same things his previous leader had done.

I was troubled because the well-being of this man was more important to me than what he could do for me as an employee. I made exceptions for him that I would not make for any other employee because I desired to see him healed.

After only two months he resigned. He felt trapped in the same situation as before. He left saying, "John, I will never work for another ministry again."

I blessed him and watched him go. We love him and his wife. The sad fact is that there is a strong call on his life for the very thing he has left, though that does not mean he won't have success in other areas.

I was troubled after he left, so I sought the Lord. "Why did he leave so quickly when both of us felt so right about it?"

A few weeks later the Lord used a wise pastor friend of mine to answer this question. "Many times God will allow people to run from situations He desires them to face if they are set on running from them in their hearts."

I 'm often asked, "When should I leave a church or ministry team? How bad does it have to get?"

I respond, "Who sent you to the church you presently attend?"

The majority of the time people answer, "God did."

"If God sent you," I reply, "do not leave until God releases you. If the Lord is silent, He is often saying, 'Don't change a thing. Do not leave. Stay where I have placed you!'"

When God does instruct you to leave, you will go out with peace, no matter what the condition of the ministry. "For ye shall go out with joy, and be led forth with peace" (Isa. 55:12, KJV). Therefore, your departure will not be based on the actions or behavior of others but rather on the Spirit's leading. So leaving a ministry is not based on how bad things are.

To leave with an offended or critical spirit is not the plan of God. It is reacting rather than acting on His guidance. Romans 8:14 says, "For as many as are led by the Spirit of God, these are sons of God." Notice it does not say, "For as many as react to difficult situations, these are sons of God."

Almost every time the word *son* is used in the New Testament, it comes from the Greek word *teknon* or the word *huios*. A good definition for the word *teknon* is "one who is a son by mere fact of birth."[1]

When my son Addison was born, he was John Bevere's son by the mere fact that he came from my wife and me. When he was in the nursery in the midst of all the other newborns, you could not recognize him as my son by personality. When friends and family came to visit, they could not pick him out except by the nametag above his crib. He did not possess anything that set him apart. Addison would be considered a *teknon* of John and Lisa Bevere.

We find *teknon* used in Romans 8:15–16. It says that because we have received the spirit of adoption, "the Spirit Himself bears witness with our spirit that we are children [*teknon*] of God." When a person receives Jesus Christ as Lord, he is a child of God by fact of the new birth experience. (See John 1:12.)

The other Greek word translated *son* in the New Testament is *huios*. Many times it is used in the

New Testament to describe "one who can be identified as a son because he displays the character or characteristics of his parents."[2]

As my son Addison grew, he started looking and acting like his father. When Addison was six, Lisa and I took a trip and left him with my parents. My mother told my wife that Addison was almost a carbon copy of his daddy. His personality was like mine when I was his age. As he has grown, he has become more like his dad. He now can be recognized as John Bevere's son not only by the fact of his birth, but also by characteristics and personality that resemble his father's.

Immature Christians are less likely to follow the leading of the Spirit of God.

So, to put it simply, the Greek word *teknon* means "babies or immature sons." The Greek word *huios* is most often used to describe "mature sons."[3]

Looking at Romans 8:14 again, we read, "For as many as are led by the Spirit of God, these are sons [*huios*] of God." We can see clearly that it is the mature sons who are led by the Spirit of God. Immature Christians are less likely to follow the leading of the Spirit of God. Most often they react or respond emotionally or intellectually to circumstances they face. They have not yet learned to act only on the Spirit of God's leading.

As Addison grows, he will progress in character development. The more mature he becomes, the more responsibility I will entrust to him. It is wrong for him to stay immature. Likewise it is not God's will that we remain babies.

One way the character of my son Addison has grown is by facing difficult situations. When he started school he met up with some "bullies." I heard some of the things these rough kids were doing and saying to my son, and I wanted to go and deal with it. But I knew that would be wrong. For me to intervene would hinder Addison's growth.

So my wife and I continued to counsel him at home, preparing him to face the persecutions at school. He grew in character through obeying our counsel in the midst of his suffering.

This is similar to what God does with us. The Bible says, "Though He [Jesus] was a Son [*Huios*], yet He *learned obedience* by the things which He *suffered*" (Heb. 5:8, emphasis added).

Physical growth is a function of time. No two-year-old child has ever been six feet tall. Intellectual growth is a function of learning. Spiritual growth is neither a function of time or learning, but it is a function of obedience. Now look at what Peter says:

> Therefore, since Christ suffered for us in the flesh, arm yourselves also with the same mind, for *he who has suffered in the flesh has ceased from sin.*
>
> —1 Peter 4:1, emphasis added

A person who has ceased from sin is a perfectly obedient child of God. He is mature. He chooses God's ways, not his own. Just as Jesus learned obedience by the things He suffered, we learn obedience by the difficult circumstances we face. When we obey the Word of God, which is spoken by the Holy Spirit, we will grow and mature in the times of conflict and suffering. Our knowledge of Scripture is not the key. Obedience is.

Now we understand one reason why we have people in the church who have been Christians for twenty years, can quote verses and chapters of the Bible, have heard a thousand sermons and read many books, but still wear spiritual diapers. Every time they meet with difficult situations, rather than responding by the Spirit of God, they seek to protect themselves in their own way. They are "always learning and never able to come to the knowledge of the truth" (2 Tim. 3:7). They never come to the knowledge of the truth because they do not apply it.

> When we obey the Word of God, we will grow and mature in the times of conflict and suffering.

Truth must be allowed to have its way in our lives if we are going to grow and mature. It is not enough to give mental assent to it without obeying it. Even though we continue to learn, we never mature because of disobedience.

Self-Preservation

A common excuse for self-preservation through disobedience is offense. There is a false sense of self-protection in harboring an offense. It keeps you from seeing your own character flaws because the blame is deferred to another. You never have to face your role, your immaturity or your sin because you see only the faults of the offender. Therefore, God's attempt to develop character in you by this opposition is now abandoned. The offended person will avoid the source of the offense and eventually flee, becoming a spiritual vagabond.

Recently a woman told me about a friend of hers who left one church and began attending another. She invited the new pastor over for dinner. In the course of the conversation the pastor asked why she left the first church. The lady told him about all the problems in the leadership of her previous church.

The pastor listened and attempted to comfort her. From experience I know it would have been wise for that pastor to encourage the woman by the Word of God to deal with her hurt and critical attitude. If necessary, he should have suggested that she return to her former church until God released her in peace.

When we retain an offense in our hearts, we filter everything through it.

When God releases you in peace, you will not have pressure to justify your departure to others. You will not be under pressure to judge or critically expose the problems your previous church had. I knew it would only be a matter of time before she would respond to this new pastor and his leadership in the same manner she had her previous one. When we retain an offense in our hearts, we filter everything through it.

There is an old parable that fits this situation. Back in the days when the settlers were moving to the West, a wise man stood on a hill outside a new Western town. As the settlers came from the East, the wise man was the first person they met before coming to the settlement. They asked eagerly what the people of the town were like.

He answered them with a question: "What were the people like in the town you just left?"

Some said, "The town we came from was wicked. The people were rude gossips who took advantage of innocent people. It was filled with thieves and liars."

The wise man answered, "This town is the same as the one you left."

They thanked the man for saving them from the trouble they had just come out of. They then moved on further west.

Then another group of settlers arrived and asked the same question: "What is this town like?"

The wise man asked again, "What was the town like where you came from?"

These responded, "It was wonderful! We had dear friends. Everyone looked out for the others' interest. There was never any lack because all cared for one another. If someone had a big project, the entire community gathered to help. It was a hard decision to leave, but we felt compelled to make way for future generations by going west as pioneers."

The wise old man said to them exactly what he had said to the other group: "This town is the same as the one you left."

These people responded with joy, "Let's settle here!"

How they viewed their past relations was their scope for their future ones.

The way you leave a church or a relationship is the way you will enter into your next church or relationship. Jesus said in John 20:23, "If you forgive the sins of any, they are forgiven them; if you retain the sins of any, they are retained."

We preserve the sins of other people when we pick up an offense and harbor resentment. If we leave a church or a relationship resentful and embittered, we will enter into the next church or relationship with that same attitude. It will then be easier to leave our next relationship when problems arise. We are not only dealing with the hurts that took place in the new relationship, but also with the hurts from our former relationship.

Statistics say 60 to 65 percent of divorced people end up getting divorced again after remarrying.[4] The manner in which a person leaves their first marriage determines the path into their second marriage. The unforgiveness they hold against their first mate hinders their future for their second one. In blaming the other they are blind to their own role or faulty characteristics. To make matters worse, now they have the added fear of being hurt. As I said earlier, acquiring an offense keeps you from seeing your own character flaws because blame is deferred to another.

> We preserve the sins of other people when we pick up an offense and harbor resentment.

This principle is not limited to marriage and divorce. It can apply to all relationships. The pastor who helped me to understand the problem with the couple who came to my church from another, and subsequently left my church for the same reasons they had left the first, reminded me of a Bible story where a similar thing had happened.

He relayed the story of Elijah, who ran from Jezebel (1 Kings 18–19). Elijah had just executed the evil prophets of Baal and Asherah. They were the men who had led the nation into idolatry and had eaten at Jezebel's table. When Jezebel heard this, she threatened to kill Elijah within twenty-four hours.

God wanted Elijah to confront her, but instead he ran. He was so discouraged that he prayed to die. He was in no condition to fulfill the assignment. God sent an angel to feed him with two cakes and allowed him to run for forty days and nights to Mount Horeb.

When he arrived, the first thing God asked him was, "What are you doing here, Elijah?"

This seemed like a strange question. The Lord gave him food for the journey, allowing him to go, only to ask him when he arrived, "What are you doing here?" God knew Elijah was set on escaping the difficult situation. So He allowed it, though it is obvious from His question that it wasn't His original plan.

He then said to Elijah, "Go, return on your way to the Wilderness of Damascus; and when you arrive, anoint...Jehu the son of Nimshi as king over Israel. And Elisha the son of Shaphat of Abel

Meholah you shall anoint as prophet in your place" (1 Kings 19:15–16). Under Elisha's and Jehu's ministries this wicked queen and her evil system were destroyed (2 Kings 9–10). This assignment was not completed by Elijah, but by the successors God told him to anoint in his place.

The pastor said to me, "If we are so set in our hearts not to face difficult situations, God will actually release us even though it is not His perfect will."

There is an incident in Numbers 22 that illustrates this same point. Balaam wanted to curse Israel because there were great rewards in it for him personally.

The first time Balaam asked the Lord if he could go, God showed him that it was not His will for Balaam to go. When the princes of Moab returned with more money and honor, Balaam went to God again. It is ridiculous to think God's mind would now change because more money and honor were in it for Balaam. But this time God said to go with them.

Now why did God change His mind? The answer is that God did *not* change His mind. Balaam was so set on going that God let him go.

That is why His anger was aroused against Balaam when he did go.

We can pester the Lord regarding something for which He has already shown us His will. He will then allow us to do what we want although it is against His original plan—even when it is not in our best interest.

Often God's plan causes us to face hurts and attitudes we haven't been willing to face. Yet we run from the very thing that will bring strength to our lives. Refusing to deal with an offense will not free us from the problem. It will only give us temporary relief. The root of the problem remains untouched.

My experience with the young man that I hired also taught me a lesson about offenses and relationships. It is impossible to establish a healthy relationship with a person who has left another relationship bitter and offended. Healing must take place. Even though he kept saying he had forgiven his former leader, it was not forgotten.

Love forgets wrongs so that there is hope for the future. If we have truly overcome an offense, we earnestly seek to make peace. The time may not be at immediately, but in our hearts we will watch for an opportunity for restoration.

A wise friend said later, "There is an old proverb that states, 'Once a dog has been scalded with boiling water he will even fear cold water.'" How many today are afraid of the cold water that will bring refreshing because they have been burned once and cannot forgive?

Jesus desires to heal our wounds. But often we do not let Him heal them because it is not the easiest road to take. It is the path of humility and self-denial that leads to healing and spiritual maturity. It is the decision to make another's well-being more important than your own, even when that person has brought you great sorrow.

Pride cannot travel this path, but only those who desire peace at the risk of rejection. It is a trail that leads to humiliation and abasement. It is the road that leads to life.

Adapted from *The Bait of Satan*, 61–69.

THREE

Build on the Sure Foundation

DEVELOPING
Inner Strength

Ionce had an unmarried secretary who was happily dating a young man who also worked for the church. They were growing closer day by day. Everyone could see this relationship was going to end up in marriage. They were already discussing it seriously.

One Sunday night the senior pastor called them out and said, "Thus saith the Lord, you two will be married."

The next morning my secretary walked into the office on clouds. She was so excited. She asked if I would marry them, and I said I would be honored to. I set up an appointment to meet with them for counseling.

But I was uneasy. When they came into my office, my spirit was troubled. I looked at my secretary and asked if she knew this young man was the one God had selected for her. She responded with an enthusiastic, definite yes.

I then looked at him and asked, "Do you believe it is the will of God for you to marry this girl?"

He looked at me with his mouth half open for a moment, then dropped his head and shook it as if to say, "No, I am not sure."

I looked at them both and then spoke to the young man. "I will not marry you. I don't care who prophesied over you or what was said. I don't care how many have said, 'You two make a lovely couple.' If God has not revealed His will in your heart, you have no business going on with this marriage.

"If you marry without God's revealing this as His perfect will to you," I continued, "when storms come—and they will come—you will have questions: 'What if I had married another girl? Would I have had these problems? I should have made sure it was God's will. I feel trapped.'

"Then your heart will grow weary, and you will not be able to fight against the adversity that blows against your marriage. You will be a double-minded man and unstable in all your ways."

I sent them off and said there would be no reason to meet again. He was relieved. She was very upset. For the next week it was very uncomfortable in our office. But I knew I had spoken the truth. This was a time of testing for her. If God had truly spoken to her that this man was her husband, she would have to trust the Lord to reveal it to him and stay free from offense with me as well as with God. I told her to back off and let him have room to hear from God. She did.

Three weeks passed, and they requested another meeting. I immediately felt a sense of joy. This time when they came into the office, he looked at me with a sparkle in his eyes and said, "I know beyond any doubt that this is the woman God has given me to marry!" They were married seven months later.

When you know God has put you in a relationship or a church, the enemy will have a much more difficult time getting you out. You are founded on the revealed Word of God and will work through the conflicts even when it looks impossible.

Whoever believes will not act hastily" (Isa. 28:16). A person who acts hastily is an unstable person because his actions are not properly founded. This person is easily moved and swayed by the storms of persecutions and trials. For example, let's look at what happened with Simon Peter.

Jesus had entered the region of Caesarea Philippi and asked His disciples, "Who do men say that I, the Son of Man, am?" (Matt. 16:13).

Several disciples enthusiastically shared the opinion of the crowds about who Jesus was. Jesus waited until they finished, then He looked at them and asked them point-blank, "But who do you say that I am?" (v. 15).

I'm sure there was a confused, fearful look on most of the disciples' faces as they pondered this, mouths half open and speechless.

Suddenly the men who were so eager to speak, airing others' opinions, were silenced. Perhaps they had never seriously asked this question of themselves. Whatever the case, they now realized they had no answer.

Jesus did what He does so well. He located their

hearts with a question. He brought them to a true realization of what they did and did not know. They were living off the speculations of others rather than establishing in their own hearts who Jesus really was. They had not confronted themselves.

Simon, who was renamed Peter by Jesus, was the only one of the disciples who could answer. He blurted out, "You are the Christ, the Son of the living God" (v. 16).

Jesus then responded to him by saying, "Blessed are you, Simon Bar-Jonah, for flesh and blood has not revealed this to you, but My Father who is in heaven" (v. 17).

Jesus was explaining to Simon Peter the source for this revelation. Simon Peter had not received this knowledge by hearing the opinions of others or by what he was taught, but God had revealed it to him.

Simon Peter was very hungry for the things of God. He asked the most questions. It was he who walked on water while the other eleven watched. He was a man who would not settle for someone else's opinion! He wanted to hear directly from the mouth of God.

This revealed knowledge of Jesus did not come by his senses, but it was a gift, illuminated in his heart in response to his hunger. Many had seen and witnessed what Simon Peter saw and witnessed, but their hearts were not as hungry to know the will of God as was Peter's.

First John 2:27 says, "But the anointing which you have received from Him abides in you, and you do not need that anyone teach you; but as the same anointing teaches you concerning all things, and is true, and is not a lie, and just as it has taught you..."

This anointing was teaching Simon Peter. He heard what everyone else had to say, then he looked inward to what God had revealed. Once you receive revealed knowledge from God, no one can sway you. When God reveals something to you, it doesn't matter what the whole world says. They cannot change your heart.

Jesus then said to Simon Peter and the rest of the disciples, "On this rock [of knowledge revealed by God] I will build My church, and the gates of [hell] shall not prevail against it" (Matt. 16:18). So we see clearly that there is a sure foundation in the revealed Word of God; in this case it was Peter's understanding that Jesus was the Son of God.

The Illuminated Word

I have often told congregations and individuals when I am preaching to listen for God's voice within my voice. So often we are so busy taking notes that we only record everything that is said. This yields a mental understanding of the Scriptures and their interpretations—head knowledge.

When we possess solely a head knowledge two things can happen: 1) We are easily susceptible to hype or emotionalism, or 2) we are bound by our intellect. But this is not the sure foundation on which Jesus builds His church. He said it would be founded on the revealed Word, not just memorized verses.

When we listen to an anointed minister speak or when we read a book, we should look for the words or phrases that explode in our spirits. This is the Word God is revealing to us. It conveys light and spiritual understanding. As the psalmist said, "The entrance of Your words gives light; it gives understanding to the simple" (Ps. 119:130). It is the entrance of His Word into our hearts—not minds—that illuminates and clarifies. What we learn in the presence of God cannot be learned in the presence of men.

Jesus compared the unveiled Word of God to a rock. A rock speaks of stability and strength.

Often a minister may be speaking on one subject, yet God is illuminating something totally different in my own heart. On the other hand, God may anoint the exact words of that minister, and they explode within me. Either way it is the revealed Word of God to me. This is what changes us from being simple (void of understanding) to being mature (filled with understanding). This illuminated Word in our hearts is the foundation upon which Jesus said His church would be grounded.

Jesus compared the unveiled Word of God to a rock. A rock speaks of stability and strength. We recall the parable of the two houses, one built on rock and the other on sand. When adversity—such as persecution, tribulation and affliction—stormed against both houses, the one built on sand was destroyed, while the house built on rock stood.

Some things we need to hear from God cannot be found in the Bible. For example, whom should we marry? Where should we work? What church should we join? The list goes on. We must have the revealed Word of God for these decisions. Without it our decisions are founded on unstable ground.

What God reveals by His Spirit cannot be taken from us. This must be the foundation of all we do. Without it we will be easily offended by trials and tribulations that blindside us.

Recall what Jesus said about the Word being heard and received with excitement, yet not taking root in our hearts. It was received with gladness in the mind and emotions.

> Who, when they have heard the word, immediately receive it with gladness; and have *no root* in themselves, and so endure but for a time: afterward, when affliction or

persecution ariseth for the word's sake, immediately they are *offended.*

—MARK 4:16–17, KJV, EMPHASIS ADDED

We can easily interchange the words *root* and *foundation* for they both indicate the stabilizer and source of strength for a plant or structure. A person who is not stabilized or founded in the revealed Word of God is a prime candidate to be moved along by the storm of offense.

How many are just like the disciples Jesus confronted. They live on what they have heard others say or preach. The opinions and statements of others are taken as truth without seeking the counsel or witness of the Spirit. We can only live and proclaim what is revealed to us by God. This is what Jesus builds His church on.

The Solid Rock

The revealed Word of God is the solid rock on which we are to build our lives and ministries. Numerous people have told me of the many churches or ministry teams they have been a part of in only a short time. My heart grieves as I see how they are moved by trials and not by God's direction. They extol how wrong things are or how badly they and others were treated. They feel justified in their decisions. But their reasoning is only another layer of deception that keeps them from seeing the offense and their own character flaws.

They describe their present relation to the ministries or churches they are now part of as "temporary" or "this is where God has me for now." I even heard one man say, "I'm on loan to this church." They make these statements so that, if things get difficult, they have an escape route. They have no foundation to stand on in the new places they go. Storms can blow them easily to the next port.

"Where Could We Go?"

To return to the example where Jesus asks His disciples who they say He is, we see the stability that comes when you know the revealed will of God. Look at Simon Peter.

After Simon told what the Father revealed to his heart, Jesus said, "And I also say to you that you are Peter, and on this rock I will build My church, and the gates of Hades shall not prevail against it" (Matt. 16:18).

Jesus changed Simon's name to Peter. This is significant, for the name *Simon* means "to hear."[1] The name *Peter* (the Greek word *petros*) means "a stone."[2] As a result of hearing the revealed Word of God in his heart, he became a stone. A house built of stones on the solid foundation of a rock will endure the storms that beat against it.

> As we seek Him who is the living Word of God, He will be revealed, and we will be established.

The word *rock* in this verse comes from the Greek word *petra,* which means "a large rock."[3] Jesus was saying to Simon Peter that he was now made of the substance on which the house was to be founded.

Peter later wrote in his epistle, "You also, as living stones, are being built up a spiritual house" (1 Pet. 2:5). A stone is a small piece of a large rock. Strength, stability and power are in the rock of the revealed Word of God, and there is fruit in the life of a person who receives it. That person is made strong with the strength of the One who is the living Word of God, Jesus Christ.

As the apostle Paul writes in 1 Corinthians 3:11, "For no other foundation can anyone lay than that which is laid, which is Jesus Christ." As we seek Him who is the living Word of God, He will be revealed, and we will be established.

During the last days of Jesus' walk on earth, life became more difficult for His ministry team. The religious leaders and the Jews were persecuting Jesus, seeking to kill Him (John 5:16). When things started looking up and the people wanted to take Him by force and make Him king, He refused and walked away (John 6:15).

"Why did He do that?" His disciples asked themselves. "This was His opportunity, and ours." They were getting troubled. The storms were blowing hard.

"We have left our families and jobs to follow this man. We have a lot at stake. We believe He's the coming One. After all, John the Baptist declared it, and we heard Simon Peter say it in Caesarea Philippi. Those are two witnesses. But why does He keep irritating the existing leaders? Why is He digging His own grave? Why does He make such hard statements as 'O faithless and perverse generation, how long shall I be with you?' to us, His own disciples?"

The offense was beginning to mount in these men who had left all to follow Him.

Then the ultimate happened. Jesus preached something to them that sounded like flat-out heresy: "Most assuredly, I say to you, unless you eat the flesh of the Son of Man and drink His blood, you have no life in you" (John 6:53).

What is He preaching now? they wondered. *This is too far out for me! Not only that, but He said these things in front of the leaders in the synagogue in Capernaum.* For these disciples this was the straw that broke the camel's back!

> Therefore many of His disciples, when they heard this, said, "This is a hard saying; who can understand it?"
>
> —John 6:60

Notice the response of Jesus:

> When Jesus knew in Himself that His disciples complained about this, He said to

them, "Does this offend you?"

—JOHN 6:61

These are His own disciples! He does not retract the truth but instead confronts these men. He knows some have been living on a faulty foundation. He exposes that foundation and gives them an opportunity to see their own hearts. But they were not like Simon Peter or the other disciples who hungered for the truth. Look at their reaction:

> From that time *many* of His disciples went back and walked with Him no more.
>
> —JOHN 6:66, EMPHASIS ADDED

Notice it was not a few—it was "many." No doubt some were the same ones who were so quick to say earlier in Caesarea Philippi, "Some say John the Baptist, some Elijah, and others Jeremiah or one of the prophets" (Matt. 16:14). They were not founded on the revealed Word of God.

The offense built to the point where they did what many do today—they left. They thought they had been deceived and mistreated, but they were not. They did not see truth because their eyes were focused on their own selfish desires.

Now look at what happens with Simon Peter as

Jesus confronted the twelve:

> Then Jesus said to the twelve, "Do you also
> want to go away?" But Simon Peter
> answered Him, "Lord, to whom shall we
> go? You have the words of eternal life. Also
> we have come to believe and know that *You
> are the Christ, the Son of the living God.*"
> —JOHN 6:67–69, EMPHASIS ADDED

Jesus didn't beg these men, "Please don't leave. I
just lost most of My staff. How would I get along
without you?" No, He confronts them. "Do you
also want to go away?"

Notice how Simon Peter answers, even though he
is wrestling with the same opportunity to be
offended as the others. "Lord, to whom shall we go?"

What he heard must have confused him, but
there was a knowing in him that the others didn't
possess. At Caesarea Philippi, Peter had a revelation of who Jesus really was: "…the Son of the living God" (Matt. 16:16).

Now, in the heat of this trial, he spoke what was
rooted in his heart: "We have come to believe and
know that *You are the Christ, the Son of the living
God.*" These are the exact words he blurted out in

Caesarea Philippi. He was a stone, set on the established rock of the living Word of God. He would not leave offended.

Reaction Under Pressure

I often say that trials and tests *locate* a person. In other words, they determine where you are spiritually. They reveal the true condition of your heart. How you react under pressure is how the *real you* reacts.

You can have a house built on sand that is five stories high and beautiful, decorated with the most elaborate materials and craftsmanship. As long as the sun is shining, it looks like a bulwark of strength and beauty.

Next to that house you can have a single-story plain house. It is almost unnoticeable and possibly unattractive compared to the beautiful edifice next to it. But it is built on something you can't see—a rock.

As long as no storms strike, the five-story house looks much nicer. But when it encounters a severe storm, the five-story house collapses and is ruined. It may survive a few minor storms, but not the hurricane. The plain, one-story structure survives. The larger the house, the harder and more note-worthy its fall.

Some people in the church are like the disciples who were so quick to speak in Caesarea Philippi, but only later to be exposed. They may look like five-story Christians, the picture of strength, stability and beauty. They may weather a few minor and midsize storms. But when a mighty storm blows in, they are relocated.

Be sure that you build your life on God's revealed Word, not what others say. Keep seeking the Lord and listening to your heart. Don't do or say things just because everyone else does. Seek Him and stand on what is illuminated in your heart!

Adapted from *The Bait of Satan*, 71–82.

FOUR

Allow God's Sifting

DEVELOPING
Inner Strength

Simon Peter could no longer boast of being great. He had lost his natural confidence. He saw all too clearly the futility of his own strong will. He had been humbled. He was now a perfect candidate for the grace of God. God gives His grace to the humble. Humility is a prerequisite. It was a lesson burned in the conscience of Peter as he wrote in his epistle: "Be clothed with humility, for 'God resists the proud, but gives grace to the humble'" (1 Pet. 5:5).

Peter had been shaken to the verge of giving up. We know this by the message the angel of the Lord gave to Mary Magdalene at the tomb: "But go, tell His disciples—*and Peter*—that He is going before you into Galilee; there you will see Him, as He said to you" (Mark 16:7, emphasis added). The angel had to single him out. Peter was at the point of shipwreck, but God still had laid a foundation in him. It would not be removed by the shaking, but strengthened.

Jesus not only forgave Peter, but He also restored him. Now that he had been shaken, he was ready to become one of the central figures in the church. He courageously proclaimed the resurrection of Christ before the very ones responsible for His crucifixion. He faced the council, not a servant girl. With great authority and boldness he stood up to them.

History reports that Peter was crucified upside down after many years of faithful service.[1] He insisted he was unworthy to die the same death his Lord had died, so they hung him upside down. He was no longer afraid. He was a stone built on a solid foundation of the Rock.

On the night He was betrayed, Jesus was seated with His twelve apostles, giving thanks and serving communion, when He made a startling statement: "Behold, the hand of My betrayer is with Me on the table. And truly the Son of Man goes as it has been determined, but woe to that man by whom He is betrayed!" (Luke 22:21–22). What an announcement! We would say today that Jesus had "dropped a bomb" with those words.

Although Jesus knew from the beginning that He would be betrayed, it was the first time His disciples had heard of it. Can't you imagine the horrible feeling in the room as He said that one of them who had been with Him from the start, a close associate, was going to betray Him?

In response, "they began to question among themselves, which of them it was who would do this thing" (v. 23). They were overwhelmed with shock that one of them would be capable of such a horrifying thing. But their motive for this investigation was not pure. By the time their conversation ended, they had revealed that their reason for the inquest was selfish and full of pride. Look at the very next verse of Scripture:

> Now there was also a dispute among them,
> as to which of them should be considered
> the greatest.
>
> —Luke 22:24

Picture this: Jesus told them He was about to be turned over to the chief priests to be condemned to death and delivered to the Romans to be mocked, scourged and killed. The one who would do this was sitting with Him at the table.

The disciples questioned who it was, and it ended up in an argument about which of them would be the greatest. It was dishonorable—almost like children arguing over an inheritance. There was no concern for Jesus, just a jockeying for power and position. What unimaginable selfishness!

If I had been in Jesus' position, I might have asked if they had heard what I had said or if they even cared. We see from this incident an example of how the Master walked in love and patience. Most of us, if in Jesus' place, would have said, "Every one of you, get out! I am in my greatest hour of need, and you're thinking of yourselves!" What an opportunity to become offended!

We can almost guess who initiated the dispute among the disciples—Simon Peter, since he had the most dominating personality of the group and was usually the one who spoke up first.

He was probably quick to remind the others how he had been the only one to walk on water. Or perhaps he refreshed them about how he had had the first revelation of who Jesus really was. Then he may have shared again his experience on the mount of transfiguration with Jesus, Moses and Elijah.

He was fairly confident that he was the greatest of the twelve. But this confidence was not rooted in love. Rather it was anchored in pride.

Jesus looked at all of them and told them they were acting as mere men, not sons of the kingdom: "The kings of the Gentiles exercise lordship over them, and those who exercise authority over them are called 'benefactors.' But not so among you; on the contrary, he who is greatest among you, let him be as the younger, and he who governs as he who serves. For who is greater, he who sits at the table, or he who serves? Is it not he who sits at the table? Yet I am among you as the One who serves" (Luke 22:25–27).

The Purpose of Sifting

Even though Simon Peter had received abundant revelation of who Jesus was, he was not yet walking in the character and humility of Christ. He was building his life and ministry with past victories and pride. Paul admonished us to take heed how we build on our foundation in Christ (1 Cor. 3:10).

Simon Peter was not building with the materials necessary for the kingdom of God but with supplies such as a strong will and personal confidence. Though unaware, he was still awaiting the transformation of his character. His reference was from the "pride of life" (1 John 2:16).

> Paul admonished us to take heed how we build on our foundation in Christ.

Pride would never be strong enough to equip him to fulfill his destiny in Christ. If not removed, this pride would eventually destroy him. Pride was the same character flaw found in Lucifer, God's anointed cherub, causing his downfall (Ezek. 28:11–19).

Now look at what Jesus says to Simon Peter:

> And the Lord said, "Simon, Simon! Indeed, Satan has asked for you, that he may sift you as wheat."
>
> —LUKE 22:31

Pride opened the door for the enemy to come in and sift Simon Peter. The word *sift* is translated from the Greek word *siniazo*. It means "to sift, shake in a sieve; by inward agitation to try one's faith to the verge of overthrow."[2]

Now if Jesus had had the mentality many have in the church, He would have said, "Let's pray, guys, and bind this attack of the devil. We are not going to let Satan do this to our beloved Simon!" But look at what He says:

> But I have prayed for you, that your faith should not fail; and when you have returned to Me, strengthen your brethren.
>
> —LUKE 22:32

Jesus did not pray that Simon Peter would escape this intense shaking to the point of overthrow. He prayed that his faith would not fail in the process.

Jesus knew that out of this trial would emerge a new character, the one Simon Peter needed to fulfill his destiny and strengthen his brethren.

Satan had requested permission to shake Simon Peter so severely that he would lose his faith. The enemy's intent was to destroy this man of great potential who had received so much revelation. But God had a different purpose for the shaking, and as always, God is way ahead of the devil. He allowed the enemy to do this in order to shake everything in Simon Peter that *needed* to be shaken. When the enemy shakes, it is to destroy. But God has a different purpose.

God showed my wife, Lisa, five purposes for shaking an object:

1. To bring it closer to its foundation
2. To remove what is dead
3. To harvest what is ripe
4. To awaken
5. To unify or mix together so it can no longer be separated

Any thought process or heart attitude that is rooted in selfishness or pride will be purged. As a result of this tremendous shaking, all of Simon

Peter's self-confidence would be gone, and all that would remain was God's sure foundation. He would be awakened to his true condition, the dead would be removed and the ripe fruit harvested, bringing him closer to his true foundation. He would no longer function independently but would be inter-dependent on the Lord.

Peter boldly countered Jesus' words: "Lord, I am ready to go with You, both to prison and death." This statement was not born of the Spirit but out of his own self-confidence. He could not see the foreshadowing of this shaking.

Judas vs. Simon

Some think Peter was a big talker and cowardly. But in the garden, when the temple guard came to arrest Jesus, Peter unsheathed his sword and struck the high priest's servant, cutting off his right ear (John 18:10). Not many cowards attack when they are outnumbered by enemy soldiers. So he was strong, but his strength was in his own personality, not in God's humility, for the sifting had not yet begun.

It happened just as Jesus predicted. The same bold, strong Simon Peter, ready to die for Jesus, wielding the sword in the garden full of soldiers, was confronted by a little servant girl. He was intimidated by her and denied even knowing Jesus.

Some think it is the big things that cause men to stumble. Often it is the minor ones that shake us the most. This shows the futility of self-confidence.

Then Peter denied Jesus two more times. Immediately the rooster crowed, and Peter left and wept bitterly. He was shaken of all his self-confidence and believed he could never rise again. All he had left, though he was not even aware of it, was what was revealed to him by the Spirit.

Simon Peter and Judas were similar in many ways, including the fact that they both rejected Jesus in the crucial last days of Jesus' life. Yet the two men had a fundamental difference.

Judas never longed to know Jesus in the manner that Simon did. Judas was not founded in Him. It appeared that he loved Jesus since he had left all to follow Him, traveled in His constant companion-ship and even stayed under the heat of persecu-tion. He cast out devils, healed the sick and preached the gospel. (Recall that Jesus sent out the *twelve* to preach, heal and deliver—not the eleven.) But his sacrifices were not out of love for Jesus or out of a revelation of who He was.

Judas had his own agenda from the start. He never repented of his self-seeking motives. His character was revealed by statements such as: "What are you willing *to give me* if I…" (Matt. 26:14, emphasis added). He lied and flattered to gain advantage (v. 25). He took money from the treasury of Jesus' ministry for personal use (John 12:4–6). And the list goes on. He never knew the Lord even though he spent three and a half years in His company.

Both men were sorry for what they had done. But Judas did not have the foundation Peter had. Because he never hungered to know Jesus, Jesus was not revealed to him. If Judas had had a revelation of Jesus, he never could have betrayed Him. When a strong storm attacked his life, everything was shaken and blown away! See what happened:

> Then Judas, His betrayer, seeing that He had been condemned, was *remorseful* and brought back the thirty pieces of silver to the chief priests and elders, saying, *"I have sinned by betraying innocent blood."* And they said, "What is that to us? You see to it!" Then he threw down the pieces of silver in

the temple and departed, and went and
hanged himself.
—MATTHEW 27:3–5, EMPHASIS ADDED

He was remorseful and knew he'd sinned. But
he did not know the Christ. He had no understanding of the magnitude of his betrayal. He only
said, "I have betrayed innocent blood." If he had
known the Christ as Simon Peter did, he would
have gone back to Him and repented, knowing the
goodness of the Lord. Committing suicide was yet
another act of living independently of God's grace.
The shaking revealed Judas had no foundation,
even after following the Master for three years.

If Judas had had a revelation of Jesus, he never could have betrayed Him.

Numerous converts have prayed a "sinner's
prayer," attended church, become active and studied
their Bibles. All of this, however, is without a revelation of who Jesus really is, though they confess Him
with their mouths. When a severe disappointment

occurs, they are offended with God and will have nothing to do with Him.

"God never did anything for me!" I've heard them say. "I tried Christianity, but my life only became more miserable." Or, "I prayed and asked God to do this, and He did not do it!" They never laid their lives down for Jesus. Instead they tried to align themselves with Him for their own benefit. They served Him for what He could give them. They were easily offended. Here is Jesus' description of them:

> Who, when they have heard the word, immediately receive it with gladness; and have *no root in themselves,* and so endure but for a time: afterward, when affliction or persecution ariseth for the word's sake, immediately they are *offended.*
> —MARK 4:16–17, KJV, EMPHASIS ADDED

Notice that He said they were quickly offended because they had no foundation. In what are we to be rooted? We find the answer in Ephesians 3:16–18. We are to be rooted and grounded in love. Our love for God is our foundation.

Jesus said, "Greater love has no one than this,

than to lay down one's life for his friends" (John 15:13). We cannot lay down our lives for someone we do not trust. We cannot lay down our lives for God unless we know Him well enough to trust Him. We must know and understand the nature and character of God. We must have the assurance that He would never do anything to harm us.

> God is love; there is no selfishness or evil in Him. It is Satan who desires to destroy us.

He always looks out for what He knows is in our best interest. What may look like a disappointment to us will always turn out for our good if we do not lose faith. God is love; there is no selfishness or evil in Him. It is Satan who desires to destroy us.

Often we view situations in our lives through short-range glasses. This distorts the true picture. God looks at the eternal aspect of what we go through. If we look at situations only from our limited vantage, two things can happen.

First, in the midst of God's purging process we will be easy prey to offense, whether it be with God or one of His servants. Second, we can easily be deceived by the enemy. Satan will use something that seems right at the moment, but his ultimate plan is to use that to our own destruction or death. When we are settled in trusting God, we are not moved from the Father's care. We will not succumb to the temptation to care for ourselves.

Depending on God's Character

One way the enemy attempts to draw us away from trusting God is by perverting our perception of God's character. He did this in the garden with Eve when he asked her, "Has God indeed said, 'You shall *not* eat of *every tree* of the garden'?" (Gen. 3:1, emphasis added). He twisted God's commandment in order to attack and distort His character.

God had said, "Of *every tree* of the garden *you may freely eat;* but of the tree of the knowledge of good and evil you shall not eat, for in the day that you eat of it you shall surely die" (Gen. 2:16–17, emphasis added).

In essence the serpent was saying to Eve, "God is withholding everything good from you."

But God's emphasis was, "You may freely eat, except..." God had given mankind the entire garden to enjoy and all the fruit to eat with the exception of one.

The serpent was twisting the woman's perception of God by saying, "God doesn't really care for you. What good thing is He keeping back from you? He must not love you as you thought. He must not be a good God!" She was deceived and believed a lie about God's character. The desire to sin was then aroused because God's Word was no longer life but law. And "the strength of sin is the law" (1 Cor. 15:56).

The enemy still operates this way today. He perverts the character of the Father God in His children's eyes. We have all had authorities over us such as dads, teachers, bosses or governors who have been selfish and unloving. Because they are authority figures, it is easy to project their nature onto God's character since He is the ultimate authority.

The enemy has masterfully distorted the character of the Father by perverting our view of our earthly fathers. God says that before Jesus returns the hearts of the fathers will be returned to the children (Mal. 4:6). His character or nature will be seen in His leaders, and it will be a catalyst for healing.

When you know God would *never* do anything to harm or destroy you, and whatever He does or does not do in your life is in your best interest, then you will give yourself freely to Him. You will gladly be one to lay down your life for the Master.

If you have given yourself totally to Jesus and are committed to His care, you cannot be offended because you are not your own. Those who are hurt and disappointed are those who have come to Jesus for what He can do for them, not because of who He is.

When we come to Jesus merely for what He can do for us, we are easily disappointed. Self-centeredness causes us to be shortsighted. We are unable to view our immediate circumstances through the eyes of faith. When our lives are truly lost in Jesus, we know His character and share His joy. We cannot be shaken or shipwrecked.

It is easy to become offended when we judge by

our natural surroundings and circumstances.
X This is not seeing through the eyes of the Spirit.
Often God does not answer me in the manner or
amount of time I feel is absolutely necessary. But
as I look back at every case, I understand and can
see His wisdom.

To give yourself in total abandonment you must know the One who holds your life.

Occasionally our children do not understand
our methods or the logic behind their training.
We try to give explanations to the older children so
they can benefit from the wisdom. At times they
may not understand or agree because of their
immaturity. But later on in life they will. Or perhaps the reason is to test their obedience, love and
maturity. It is the same with our Father in heaven.
In these situations faith says, "I trust You even
though I don't understand."

In the epistle to the Hebrews we find the record of those who never saw the fulfillment of their promises from God and still never wavered:

> Others were tortured, not accepting deliverance, that they might obtain a better resurrection. Still others had trial of mockings and scourgings, yes, and of chains and imprisonment. They were stoned, they were sawn in two, were tempted, were slain with the sword. They wandered about in sheepskins and goatskins, being destitute, afflicted, tormented—of whom the world was not worthy. They wandered in deserts and mountains, in dens and caves of the earth. And all these, having obtained a good testimony through faith, *did not receive the promise.*
> —HEBREWS 11:35–39, EMPHASIS ADDED

They had decided God was all they wanted—no matter what the cost. They believed Him even when they died without seeing the promises fulfilled. They could not be offended!

We are rooted and grounded when we bear this intense love and trust in God. No storm, no matter how intense, can ever move us. This does not come by strong will or personality. It is a gift of grace to all who place their confidence in God, throwing away the confidence of self. But to give yourself in total abandonment you must know the One who holds your life.

Adapted from *The Bait of Satan*, 85–94.

Conclusion

As you have read this book, the Spirit of the Lord may have reminded you of relationships in the past or present in which you have held something against others. I have sensed the Lord's instruction to ask you to pray a simple prayer of release with me.

But before praying, ask the Holy Spirit to walk with you through your past, bringing before you any people against whom you have held something. Stay quiet before Him as He shows you who they are. You do not need to hunt for something that is not there. He will clearly bring them up to where you will not doubt it. As He does, you may remember the pain you experienced. Don't be afraid. He will be right there at your side comforting you.

As you release these people from blame for what they have done to you, picture each of them individually. Forgive each one personally. Cancel the debt they owe you. Then pray this prayer, but don't be limited to these words. Use this as a guideline, and be led by the Spirit of God.

> *Father, in the name of Jesus, I acknowledge that I have sinned against You by not forgiving those who have offended me. I repent of this and ask Your forgiveness.*
>
> *I also acknowledge my inability to forgive them apart from You. Therefore, from my heart I choose to forgive [insert their names—release each one individually]. I bring under the blood of Jesus all that they have done wrong to me. They no longer owe me anything. I remit their sins against me.*
>
> *Heavenly Father, as my Lord Jesus asked You to forgive those who had sinned against Him, I pray that Your forgiveness will come to those who have sinned against me.*
>
> *I ask that You will bless them and lead them into a closer relationship with Yourself. Amen.*

Now write the names of the people you have released in a journal and record that on this date you made the decision to forgive them.

You may have to exercise to stay free from the power of the negative words of offense. Make a commitment to pray for your offenders just as you would pray for yourself. Your journal will help you remember. If thoughts continue to bombard your mind, cast them down with the Word of God, and declare your decision to forgive. You have asked for God's grace to forgive, and unforgiveness is not as powerful as His grace. Be bold and fight the good fight of faith.

When you know your heart is strong and settled, go to them. Remember that you are going for the purpose of reconciliation for their benefit, not your own. By doing this you will seal the victory. You will win a brother. (See Matthew 18:15.) This is well pleasing in the sight of God. By your actions you have overcome the power of negative words in your life.

> Now to Him who is able to keep you from stumbling, and to present you faultless before the presence of His glory with exceeding joy, to God our Savior, who alone is wise, be glory and majesty, dominion and power, both now and forever. Amen.
> —JUDE 24–25

Adapted from *The Bait of Satan*, 175–177.

Notes

Chapter 2
Face Reality

1. W. E. Vine, Merrill Unger and William White, Jr., *An Expository Dictionary of Biblical Words* (Nashville, TN: Thomas Nelson, 1984), s.v. "child" (hereinafter cited as *Vine's Expository Dictionary*).

2. Vine et al., *Vine's Expository Dictionary,* s.v. "son."

3. Under the entry for "son" in *Vine's Expository Dictionary,* the author made there powerful statements about the difference between a child by birth (*teknon*) and a son by resemblance (*huios*):

   "The difference between believers as 'children of God' *teknon* and as 'sons of God' *huios* is brought out in Romans 8:14–21. The Spirit bears witness with their spirit that they are 'children of God,' and as such, they are His heirs and joint-heirs with Christ. This stresses the fact of their spiritual birth (vv. 16–17). On the other hand, 'as many as are led by the Spirit of God, these are sons of God,' i.e., 'these and no other.' Their conduct gives evidence of the dignity of their relationship and their likeness to His character.

   "The Lord Jesus used *huios* in a very significant way, as in Matthew 5:9, "Blessed are the peacemakers, for they shall be called the sons of God,' and vv. 44, 45, 'Love your enemies and pray for those who persecute you, that you may be [become] sons of your Father in heaven.' The disciples were to do these things, not in order that they might become children of God, but that, being children (note 'your Father' throughout), they might make the fact manifest in their character, might 'become sons.' See also 2 Corinthians 6:17–18."

4. The Rockford Institute, Center on the Family in America (Rockford, IL).

Chapter 3
Build on the Sure Foundation

1. *Zondervan Topical Bible* (Grand Rapids, MI: Zondervan, 1969), s.v. "Simon."
2. Vine et al., *Vine's Expository Dictionary,* s.v. "rock."
3. Ibid.

Chapter 4
Allow God's Shifting

1. J. D. Douglas et al., eds., *New Bible Dictionary,* 2nd ed., (Wheaton, IL: Tyndale House, 1982), s.v. "Peter."
2. Logos Bible Study Software for Microsoft, version 1.6 (Oak Harbor, WA: Logos Research Systems, Inc., 1993), s.v. "sift."

If you are enjoying the Inner Strength Series by
John Bevere, here are some other titles from
Charisma House that we think will minister to you…

Breaking Intimidation
Break free from the fear of man
John Bevere
ISBN: 0-88419-387-X
Retail Price: $13.99

The Bait of Satan
Don't let resentment cripple you
John Bevere
ISBN: 0-88419-374-8
Price: $13.99

Thus Saith the Lord?
How prophetic excesses have hurt the church
John Bevere
ISBN: 0-88419-575-9
Retail Price: $12.99

The Devil's Door
Recognize the trap of rebellion
John Bevere
ISBN: 0-88419-442-6
Price: $12.99

Pathway to His Presence
A 40-day devotional leading into His presence
John and Lisa Bevere
ISBN: 0-88419-654-2
Price: $16.99

The Fear of the Lord
Gain a holy fear and awe of God
John Bevere
ISBN: 0-88419-486-8
Price: $12.99

Charisma°
HOUSE
Books about Spirit-Led Living

To pick up a copy of any of these titles, contact your local Christian bookstore or order online at www.charismawarehouse.com.